ANCIENT IRAN

Bronze tripod stand for a jar, said to be from Luristan: Middle Elamite Style, *c.* 1200–900 B.C. Ht. 0·194 [1970.402] (Bomford Trust Purchase).

Fontispiece: Near life-size plaster (stucco) head of a Sasanian king, probably Bahram V (AD 420–38), from a palace at Kish in Iraq. Ht. 0·480 [1932.980].

UNIVERSITY OF OXFORD
ASHMOLEAN MUSEUM

ANCIENT IRAN

BY

P. R. S. MOOREY

OXFORD

PRINTED FOR THE VISITORS

AND SOLD AT THE ASHMOLEAN MUSEUM

1975

OTHER TITLES IN THIS SERIES
Archaeology, Artefacts and the Bible (1969)
Ancient Egypt (1970)
Ancient Cyprus (1975)

Set in Photon Times and
Printed in Great Britain at the Alden Press, Oxford

Acknowledgements

I am most grateful to Mr. James Allan, Mr. H. J. Case, Keeper of the Department of Antiquities, Dr. David Frankel and Dr. T. Cuyler Young, Jnr., for reading and commenting on a draft of this booklet. They have done much to improve its accuracy and clarity; for what has survived their scrutiny I alone am responsible. I am much indebted to Mrs. Pat Clarke for the drawings, to Miss O. Godwin for the photography and to Mrs. Patricia Baines for patiently retyping my drafts and assuring me that to at least one non-specialist they were relatively intelligible.

Notes

1. The numbers which appear in square brackets in the plate captions are the serial numbers of the objects in the accessions registers of the Department of Antiquities.

2. Measurements are given in metres or parts of a metre; Ht. = height; L. = length; W. = width and D. = diameter.

3. The rendering of Iranian place and personal names in English has yet to be fully standardised. The differences are rarely great, but the reader will regularly encounter variants.

Contents

Preface

The collection of antiquities from Iran in the Ashmolean Museum, though relatively small, is representative of all phases in her history from about 4000 BC to the Islamic Conquest. Much of the material comes from the official division of objects following excavations since 1948 by British archaeologists supported by the Museum; a practice discontinued by the Iranian authorities in 1974. These are:

Baba Jan Tepe (*Goff*, 1966–1969)

Bampur (*de Cardi*, 1966)

Geoy Tepe (*Burton Brown*, 1948)

Haftavan Tepe (*Burney*, 1968: continuing)

Kara Tepe (*Burton Brown*, 1956)

Nush-i Jan Tepe (*Stronach*, 1967: continuing)

Pasargadae (*Stronach*, 1961–1963).

Susa (*Louvre Loan*)

Tall-i Nokhodi (*Goff*, 1961–1962)

Yanik Tepe (*Burney*, 1960–1962)

Yarim Tepe (*Stronach*, 1960)

Earlier acquisitions include seals of the Achaemenid and Sasanian periods, and the first of what was to be an outstanding collection of metalwork, and some pottery, from Luristan and Gilan (*Amlash*), greatly enlarged since 1965 through the continuing generosity of Mr. J. Bomford. Many of the outstanding pieces acquired from Mr. Bomford will be found illustrated in the plates that follow.

This booklet seeks to set these objects in their wider archaeological context and at the same time present a sketch, it is no more, of the prehistory and early history of Iran: a country undeservedly less well known for its early civilisation than Egypt, or Assyria and Babylonia, whose monuments have now been familiar in Europe for nearly a century and a half. Suggestions for further reading in the subject will be found at the end of the main text.

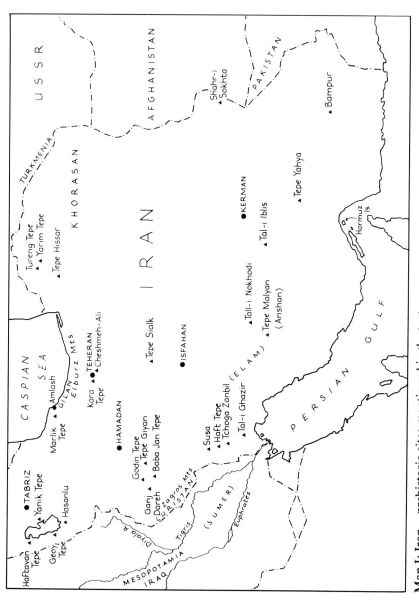

Map I: Iran—prehistoric sites mentioned in the text.

I. Introduction

(a) THE IRANIAN LEGACY

.........What have we to do
with Kaikobad the Great, or Kaikhosru?'
Fitzgerald, *Rubaiyat of Omar Khayyam*,
IX (1868; 2 nd Edition).

When television screens throughout the world in 1971 carried pictures of the Shah's celebration of the 2,500th anniversary of the founding of the Persian Empire by Cyrus the Great, few were aware of his country's origins. Today, when the Old Testament is no longer generally read, 'the law of the Medes and Persians which altereth not' (*Daniel* VI. 12) remains proverbial, but without context, whilst the lively account of the court of the Achaemenid king Xerxes (Ahasuerus) in the *Book of Esther*, if known at all, passes for a fable. Modern translations of the vivid narrative of the Greek historian Herodotus, who in the fifth century BC was the first western scholar to write systematically of Iran and the Iranians for the information of his contemporaries, somewhat restored the balance. But it is archaeology which in the last twenty-five years has offered the most reliable and fullest account of Iran's emergence as a cultural and political force in the ancient Near East.

Persian carpets, gardens and miniature paintings have long been prized and imitated in Europe. Each represents a craft whose earliest history is sadly obscured by the inevitable decay of its products. The oldest surviving Persian carpet was preserved, deep frozen, from the fourth century BC in the grave of a Scythian chieftain in the Altai region of Asiatic Russia. The ghosts of identical carpets exported westwards have been preserved on the walls of tombs in northern Greece painted in the third century BC exactly as real ones would have hung, even then much admired, on the walls of rich men's houses. Timasion, a general in the Greek army at the time of Xenophon, had a Persian carpet worth 1000 drachmae (1 drachma was the highest daily wage for a skilled

1

manual worker). Such age-old amenities of the Persian garden as porticoed pavilions, pools and canals, have been excavated at Pasargadae, created by Cyrus the Great in the sixth century BC as the capital city of his new empire. According to Xenophon, the Persian prince Cyrus the Younger astonished the Spartan Lysander (died 395 BC) when showing him his garden at Sardis, where he was governor, by saying that he had planned it all, and that when not on campaign he always gardened before dinner. Iran's varied animal life, later so much a part of her miniature painters' repertory of motifs, inspired the designs potters painted on their wares and the forms smiths cast on ornamental metalwork from earliest times (pls. I–II).

Language offers one of the most interesting indicators of the influence one culture has had on another. Behind that familiar word *magic* lies the Old Persian *magus*, the member of a priestly caste best known to the West through the three wisemen (Magi) from the East who brought offerings to the Christ child. Not only the word *bazaar* for a market is of Iranian origin, but so also are the names of such trade commodities as *shawls* and *sashes*, *turquoises* and *taffeta*, *awnings* and *tiaras*. Among fruits and vegetables *oranges*, *lemons*, *melons* and *peaches*, *spinach* and *asparagus*, in name and in origin, may be traced back to Iran. So too may *paradise*, the pleasure park of the Iranian king or aristocrat, synonymous in our tradition with the legendary garden of Eden, primeval home of unsullied human bliss. Although now concealed by successive translations the original Aramaic portions of the Old Testament contained many loan-words from Old Persian that vividly reflect those areas of human activity in which Iranian influence was most strongly felt under the Achemenid kings (*c.* 550–330 BC). Among such words are: *chief-ministers* and *counsellors*, *police-chiefs* and *corporal-punishment*, *written-order* and *message*, *belt* and *trousers*, *furnishings* and *ration*.

It is usually forgotten that Iran was also the home of a number of outstanding religious traditions, for in Europe they have too often been obscured by such misleading masterpieces as the German philosopher Nietzsche's *Also sprach Zarathustra* (1883–1884) or by dubious translations, more often paraphrases, of their sacred books. The still living cult of Zoroastrianism, with its sensitive ethical teaching, initially absorbed a vast repertory of myth and

Plate I: Three buff ware painted goblets similar to pottery from Tepe Sialk III; exact source unknown; *c.* 3200 BC. Ht. 0.132, 0.147, 0.124 [1971.978–80]. (*From the collection of Mr. James Bomford.*)

Plate II: Bronze cheekpiece for a horsebit cast as an ass or mule; Luristan; 9th to 8th centuries BC. L. 0.076 Ht. 0.079 [1951.196]. (*From the collection of the late Mr. Frank Savery.*)

3

areas have been placed on the archaeological map of Iran and often unexpected contributions to the earliest development of civilisation in the Near East revealed. All this research is slowly bringing ever better order into what was so recently no more than a mass of scattered and apparently unrelated data. In few countries has so short a period of time brought such transformations in knowledge of its antiquity.

II. The Geographical Setting

The country in English traditionally called 'Persia', after the Greek, is known to its inhabitants as 'Iran', land of the Aryans. In using this name in accounts of the country's prehistory two points must always be borne in mind. Firstly, according to present understanding, the Iranian-speaking peoples did not enter this region until sometime in the second millennium BC, and secondly, though modern Iran's political frontiers generally follow prominent geographical features, her ancient history intimately involves a number of regions to the east now politically part either of the U.S.S.R., of Afghanistan, or of Pakistan.

Iran, a country six times the size of the British Isles, has an enormously varied and often very rugged and inhospitable landscape. It has been likened in form to a bowl with a high rim enclosing an irregular and lower, but not low-lying, interior. To north and west the mountain rim is especially high and thick, whilst to the south and east, where it is lower and thinner, the sea on the one hand, extreme aridity of the land on the other, re-inforces the surrounding barrier. Lines of communication are confined to certain well-defined routes as regions favourable to settlement are so often surrounded by intractable wastes. Of these routes that from the Diyala region in Iraq through the central Zagros to the Hamadan plain and then north and eastwards, the so-called Khorasan Road, was the most crucial. The climate varies more markedly than elsewhere in the Near East, not only from region to region, but often within them. Intense heat, bitter cold, alternating calms and strong winds, and unreliable rainfall, have all left their mark on the land and its inhabitants, whether it be in the almost monsoonal conditions of Gilan or the arid wastes of Baluchistan.

Human settlement is concentrated on the lower slopes and plains of the north and west, extending through the Elburz mountains to the Caspian coastal provinces, where rainfall is sufficient for regular cultivation. In regions where irrigation is needed springs are tapped in the mountains and the water led from them to the farmland by

7

underground channels (*qanats*) reached from ground level by shafts at regular intervals. This distinctive system dates back to at least the Achaemenid period. Apart from the Karun and Kharkeh rivers there is no major river system in Iran to support irrigation as in Iraq or Egypt. Archaeological research increasingly confirms the view, reflected in the description of Iran given by Herodotus, that in antiquity settlement was more extensive than it is today—though there is no reason to suppose the overall pattern was markedly different. The prehistoric role of nomads and semi-nomads, so important in historical times, is uncertain, as tracing them archaeologically is very difficult.

In every important respect Iran is economically self-sufficient. Where conditions allow, vegetation is adequate. Of trees, the poplar is used for construction, the plane for fittings and the elm for ploughs; poorer woods provide fuel. Cypress, acacia and Turkestan elm, with lilac, jasmine and red rose adorn the gardens of Iran. Fruits are numerous and varied, pears, apples, apricots, grapes, cherries, figs, melons, pomegranates, dates and oranges; as are nuts such as almonds and pistachios. The standard cereals are widely grown. Wild animals, though not nearly as prevalent as they were, survive in sufficient numbers to remind us that in ancient Iran no subject was more popular with artists and craftsmen. Lions, tigers and bears are now rare, but wolves, leopards, lynxes, foxes and jackals, wild boar, goat and sheep, deer, gazelles and asses are commoner. Among domesticated breeds the sheep, goat, horse and ass are pre-eminent, the camel is now less often seen (pl. IV). Not only those birds poetically associated with Iran, the cock and the nightingale, but also birds-of-prey such as the eagle, vulture and hawk, and many more docile species flourish here. Iran has many raw materials particularly prized in antiquity: building, semi-precious and ornamental stones, and such metal ores as copper, iron and probably tin.

Developing archaeology bears the marks of Iran's geography. Regionalism has always played an important part in the country's history, but its role in her prehistory may at present be exaggerated by the unequal concentration of research. Western Iran, admittedly the focus of human settlement, is the best known. Here certain crucial sites offer long archaeological sequences into which evidence from more briefly occupied, or excavated, sites may be dove-tailed:

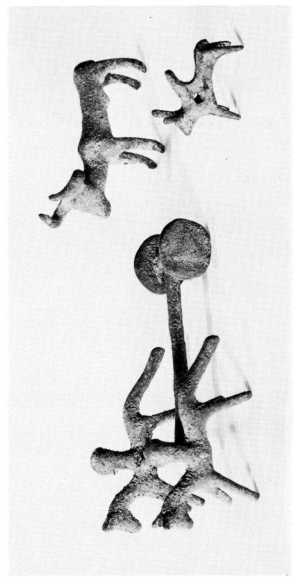

Plate IV: Bronze model cart drawn by equids with riders (L. 0·087); bronze model bull (L. 0·055); bronze zebu pendant (L. 0·025); all from Gilan, *c.* 1200–1000 BC [1967.1228, 1967.1226, 1967.1227]. (*Bomford Trust purchase.*)

Hasanlu in Azerbaijan, Godin Tepe in south Kurdistan, Tepe Giyan in Luristan, Tepe Sialk on the plateau and Susa in Khuzistan. North-eastwards Tepe Hissar provides a comparable framework, with work by Russian archaeologists in Turkmenia of increasing relevance. Southwards, and south-eastwards, the present position is more complex, since recent work at such major sites as Tepe Yahya, Shahr-i Sokhta, Tall-i Iblis, Shahdad and Bampur has yet to be fully integrated. Such also is the case in Fars, where the older excavations at Tall-i Bakun, and smaller sites, is now being greatly extended by work at Tepe Malyan, ancient Anshan.

III. Tepes, Terminology and Chronology

The sequence of events and cultures in Iran before the Achaemenid period (*c.* 550–330 BC) is inferred almost entirely from superimposed strata of debris in ancient settlement mounds. Supplementary information from cemeteries and surface surveys is useful only in so far as it may be tied into such a basic sequence. Buildings of mud, mud-brick or rubble, with plastered walls and roofs, when they collapse leave little or nothing to salvage and a newcomer will merely level off the ruins and build above them. In the course of time accumulating debris forms a mound (*tepe*, *tal*, *tell*) in which the sequence of remains can be observed, and recorded, by cutting trenches into it. Stratigraphy—observing variations in a mound's growth—enables changes in architecture, techniques (potting, metalworking etc.) and domestic equipment to be placed in order of time and related to observed interruptions or changes of settlement. Distinctive types of pottery, more rarely of other objects, allow for the correlation of levels on one mound with those of others.

In Iran, where correlation with the historical chronologies of Mesopotamia and, more rarely, Elam are only of very restricted use, Carbon-14 (measurements of residual radioactivity in carbon specimens) has provided an invaluable source of absolute chronology in recent years. Despite its acknowledged uncertainties, it increasingly offers an indispensable framework for study. Unfortunately no chronological terminology has yet been devised which registers unambiguously the complex and differential growth of regional cultures in Iran. Not even the terms broadly signifying technological stages, Neolithic, Chalcolithic, Bronze and Iron, used elsewhere, are always applied here. For the present relative chronology is commonly denoted either by the time range of a prevalent pottery type: 'Soft Ware Horizon', 'Northern Gray Ware Horizon', or by the numerically or alphabetically designated sequence of levels in a primary excavation: 'Hasanlu V', 'Geoy Tepe B'. It should be noted that in such cases the numbering may be from top to bottom of the *tepe* (i.e. late to early) as at Hasanlu or Godin

Tepe, or *vice versa* as at Tepes Hissar and Sialk. The ensuing need for elaborate, and rarely unambiguous, cross-referencing is as bewildering to the expert as to the general reader and is largely avoided in this essay.

Here the following basic scheme applies:

Early Neolithic   *c.* 9000–6000 BC (Iraq: Jarmo/Hassuna)
Late Neolithic   *c.* 6000–4000 BC (Iraq: Halaf/Early Ubaid)
Chalcolithic   *c.* 4000–3000 BC (Iraq: Late Ubaid/Uruk/Jemdet Nasr)
Early Bronze   *c.* 3000–2400 BC (Iraq: Early Dynastic)
Late Bronze   *c.* 2400–1350 BC (Iraq: Akkad/Neo-Sumerian/Old Babylonian/Kassite)
Iron I   *c.* 1350–1000 BC (Iraq: Middle Assyrian/Babylonian)
Iron II   *c.* 1000– 800 BC (Iraq: Neo-Assyrian)
Iron III   *c.* 800– 400 BC (Iraq: Neo-Assyrian/Babylonian/Achaemenid)
Iron IV   *c.* 400– 150 BC (Iraq: Late Achaemenid/Seleucid)
Parthian   *c.* 150– 250 AD (As Iran)
Sasanian   *c.* 250– 650 AD (As Iran)

IV. Hunters, Pastoralists and Farmers

Only isolated finds at widely separated sites in the Zagros mountains or along the Caspian shores mark those thousands of years when Iran was inhabited by small nomadic bands of gatherers and hunters, sometimes living in caves, sometimes camping in the open. About the tenth millennium BC under the impetus of climatic conditions less arid and warmer than today, groups of such people in the Zagros and its flanking foothills began to establish primitive villages. The earliest of these, as at Ganj Dareh (level E) in Kurdistan (about 8500 to 8000 BC) were still only temporary encampments, but were supported by intensified food collecting or simple cultivation of cereals. Sheep were soon domesticated; bone and stone industries modified to fresh purposes and clay, lightly fired from the first, increasingly used for daub, and for the manufacture of crude animal and human figurines or geometric shapes that served as gaming pieces or counters. As mastery of animal husbandry and rainfed cereal cultivation increased villages grew more elaborate. Houses were built of mudbrick with ovens and storage bins, as in Ganj Dareh (level D) about 8000 to 7500 BC. Land was systematically cleared for farming and a pattern of seasonal transhumance established between highland and lowland pastures. Crude pottery then first appeared and in time came to be tempered, slipped and burnished, or painted with simple geometric patterns in red ochre as at Tepe Guran in Luristan.

In time, minor climatic variations and population pressures stimulated agricultural expansion into previously unexploited regions. In Khuzistan, for instance, between about 7500 to 6000 BC, first simple transhumant farmers then later more permanent settlers in larger villages domesticated cattle and developed the irrigation systems without which such an area could not be farmed. Similar trends may be seen at work in Fars, on the plateau at Sialk, in Azerbaijan, in north-east Iran and in Turkmenia. To what extent these areas developed in association, or independently, remains to be seen. By at least the seventh millennium BC they were linked by a

13

Plate V: Buff ware bowl with geometric designs in dark paint from Susa in Khuzistan; *c*. 4000 BC; D. 0·180×0·200, Ht. 0·085 [Louvre Loan].

trade in raw materials and some finished products. Obsidian from Turkey, and cowrie shells from the Gulf, were used in Khuzistan from 7500 BC. The routes along which such goods travelled may also have seen the transmission from their natural habitat to new zones, of wild grain, goat and sheep for domestication. By the sixth millennium turquoise from north-east Iran, native copper from the plateau, and red ochre, perhaps from Fars or Hormuz, reached Khuzistan revealing steadily widening horizons.

V. Townsmen and Traders

By *c.* 5000–4500 BC many areas of Iran supported a variety of communities, some in nascent townships, others in small irrigation or rainfed farming villages, yet others in pastoral camps. All were closely related through the interchange of craft goods and agricultural produce for meat and animal produce. The range of raw materials regularly exploited has grown. Craft techniques in potting and metalworking may be seen to have improved with the widespread production of fine painted pottery (pls. V, VI) and of simple copper tools and weapons, and the exploitation of gold, silver and lead (pls. VIII, XI).

Plate VI: Buff ware jar painted in black with animals from Tall-i Nokhodi in Fars; *c.* 3200 BC; Ht. 0·132 [1963.1543].

15

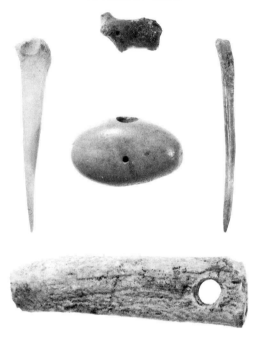

Plate VII: Baked clay model of a ram from Geoy Tepe, level 'K' (L. 0·045); two bone tools (L. 0·130), a bone hammer head (L. 0·076) and an antler tool (L. 0·160); all from Yanik Tepe; Early Bronze period [1949.990a, 1962.407, 1968.149, 1968.138, 1962.410].

As urban civilisations based on highly productive irrigation agriculture grew rapidly, but independently, in the adjacent areas of southern Iraq (Sumer) and Khuzistan (Elam) in the fourth millennium BC, demand for raw materials not available in these regions steadily expanded. It stimulated the growth in inner Iran not only of major mining and distribution centres, but also of workshops for the large-scale production of objects from locally available raw materials. Now for the first time both texts and artefacts reveal something of the course of commercial contacts between Mesopotamia and Iran, perhaps also of Elamite attempts to monopolise the valuable transit trade both north-eastwards along the great Khorasan road and eastwards through southern Iran. The early script of Elamite ('Proto-Elamite'), a language with no known relations and even in its developed form only imperfectly understood, has been found on tablets at Susa and various sites in

16

Plate VIII: Copper (?) goblet; south-west Iran; *c.* 2500–2300 BC; Ht. 0·140 [1974.26]. (*Bomford Trust purchase.*)

inner Iran. The earliest, with little more than numerical notations, are those from Godin Tepe on the Khorasan road, slightly later those at Tepe Sialk on the plateau, and at Tal-i Ghazir, Tepe Malyan and Tepe Yahya in the south.

By about 2800 BC the inhabitants of such towns as Shahr-i Sokhta, Yahya and Iblis processed, respectively, the lapis-lazuli, chlorite and copper easily accessible to them, producing for export both concentrated raw material and finished goods. In a Sumerian epic relating to the earlier third millennium BC the King of Uruk in Iraq sends grain to the Iranian state of Aratta in exchange for gold, silver and lapis-lazuli. This trade was not only land-borne, for there is increasing evidence for a sea trade between the lands of the Persian Gulf, southern Iran and the Indus region to the east, even perhaps to Egypt in the west.

VI. Elamites and Aryans

When records first reveal isolated details of Elam's history, *c.* 2700 BC, she was already involved in periodic conflict with Sumer. Under the Dynasty of Akkad (*c.* 2370–2200 BC) Mesopotamian armies and cultural influences, which were to endure for a millennium, dominated Elam. The local language, and script, were then superseded by the Akkadian language with its cuneiform script now used also to write Elamite. But Elam was never for long a docile prey; she was as ready to attack her western neighbours as they were to ravage her. The ferocious destruction of the IIIrd Dynasty of Ur by the Elamites, *c.* 2000 BC was long remembered in Mesopotamia. For most of the second millennium Elam's history remains to be written. Little relevant material has yet been revealed from excavations at such sites as Susa, Haft Tepe and Anshan. By the thirteenth century there was a marked revival under a series of masterful Elamite kings, whose buildings and building inscriptions at Susa and Tchoga Zanbil have yielded some of the best available information on Elamite culture. Then again she faded before Babylonian invaders, only to revive briefly in the eighth and seventh centuries. About 640 BC Elam was finally crushed by the Assyrian army of Ashurbanipal; but her language at least endured in the Achaemenid Empire both in royal inscriptions and in administrative texts.

Although Elamite material culture often has striking affinities to that of Babylonia (pl. X), its individual character is more and more apparent as excavations proceed. The Elamite pantheon of deities, known from texts, is quite distinct; goddesses predominate, reflecting the special place of women in Elamite society. The prevalence of demons and witches, noted in texts from Iraq, is revealed in art by monsters, half-man half-animal (Cover picture), and by fabulous composite creatures. From prehistoric times the snake played a special role in religious imagery. Even that most distinctive of Mesopotamian structures, the staged temple-tower (ziggurat) had features in Elam not found elsewhere. The sanctuary

18

on the top at Susa, shown on Assyrian reliefs, is decorated with pairs of massive animal horns, as are Elamite temples shown on prehistoric seals. Such artefacts as cylinder seals, friezes of polychrome glazed bricks and certain types of bronze weapon equally well-known in Babylonia have in Elam designs of purely local origin.

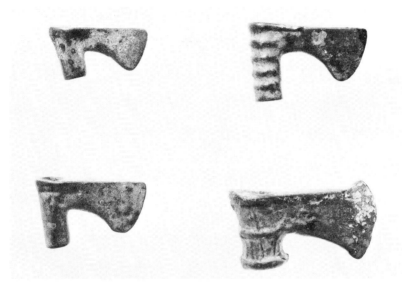

Plate IX: Bronze axeheads; Luristan; *c.* 2400–2000 BC; L. 0·079, 0·098, 0·088, 0·116 [1951.155, 153, 154, 152]. (*From the collection of the late Mr. Frank Savery.*)

The cities and communities of Iran outside Elam from *c.* 3000 to 1400 BC are still shadowy, so far represented by small building areas excavated in a few selected mounds and by a series of distinctive pottery types recovered from them and from surface surveys. These give clues, but little more, to the range and nature of contemporary relationships. In north-east Iran by about 2800 BC at sites like Yarim Tepe, Tureng Tepe and Tepe Hissar, a painted pottery style gave way to a grey-black monochrome tradition (pl. XI) which lasted for the best part of a millennium. At Hissar richly equipped graves and substantial architecture reveal a high level of mercantile enterprise and technical skill in metallurgy and stoneworking. Hissar played an important role in the westward transmission of lapis-lazuli from Afghanistan, also of more locally

19

Plate X: Base Silver (?) roller frame from western Iran; exact source and function unknown; Elamite or Babylonian; *c.* 1800–1700 BC; Ht. 0·142 [1971.25]. (*From the collection of Mr. James Bomford.*)

Plate XI: Burnished grey pottery; Yarim Tepe; later third millennium BC; Ht. 0·165, 0·084, 0·078 [1963.1519–20, 1524].

Plate XII: Dark ware jars with incised decoration and a baked clay stamp-seal (restored); Yanik Tepe, Early Bronze period; Ht. 0·107, 0·109, 0·064, 0·030 [1962.383, 388–9, 404].

available alabaster. Sometime about 1850 BC the course of events in this area was radically disrupted in circumstances yet to be unravelled, and there follows a hiatus in regular settlement until about 1400 BC.

The archaeological assemblage in western Iran is rather different. For much of the third millennium a distinctive incised monochrome grey pottery (pl. XII), originating somewhere in Caucasia or eastern Turkey, is found extending into Iran from such sites as Yanik Tepe

Plate XIII: Painted bowl (restored); Geoy Tepe, level D., *c.* 2000 BC; D. 0·160 [1949.1033].

near Lake Rezaiyah down to the Hamadan Plain and the central western Zagros. This is taken to mark a population movement southwards, parallel to a contemporary influx from eastern Turkey into Syria and Palestine, marked out by the 'Khirbet Kerak' pottery.* Late in the third millennium these dark wares were superseded by polychrome painted pottery related to the 'Khabur pottery'† of the north Syro-Mesopotamian steppe region. Here community of culture was established by the widely settled Hurrian-speaking peoples, and through a vital trade in tin westwards from unknown sources in Iran. About 1550 BC these Hurrians were forged into a briefly powerful kingdom by the intrusive Mitanni, an

* See the Ashmolean Palestinian display.
†See the Ashmolean Syrian display.

23

aristocracy of chariot warriors using Aryan names and worshipping Aryan gods like Mitra, Varuna and Indra.

The immediate source of these people, certainly to the east or north-east in Iran, and their earlier history there is tantilisingly obscure, though they were closely related, linguistically at least, to the Aryan peoples who at much the same time moved more directly southwards from west central Asia to destroy the great Indus valley civilisation. Without any known trace in the archaeological record of Iran so far, their religion and culture have been largely reconstructed by philologists from ancient collections of hymns, the *Vedas* of India and the *Yashts* of Iran. As neither is in any sense historical, and they were not written down until very long after the period in question, much remains in dispute. These western 'Indo-Aryans' may have been relatively few in number and readily absorbed by local populations, as seems to have been the eventual fate of the Mitanni. Only the subsequent arrival of the Iranian-speaking peoples led to the real transformation of the country now bearing their name.

VII. The Iranian Invasions and the Early Iron Age

Linguistic and archaeological evidence may be correlated to show that the Iranian-speaking peoples entered Iran first from the north-east and spread slowly westwards across the northern part of the country to Azerbaijan before turning southwards, in time superseding the indigeneous peoples of the Zagros valleys. It was a complex and extended series of migratory movements. Beginning *c.* 1400 BC it has been charted archaeologically from east to west

Plate XIV: Bronze horse-bell inscribed 'Property of Menua' (king of Urartu, *c.* 810–780 BC); western Iran; Ht. 0·085 [1974.357]. (*Bomford Trust purchase.*)

through the widespread use of a distinctive plain grey pottery, with ancestors in the Hissar region (pl. XI), which progressively replaced the painted wares of the Later Bronze Age in the west. Iron remains very rare, even at the end of Iron Age I, dated to about 1000 BC.

In the two centuries after 1000 BC (Iron Age II) iron came into widespread use and more marked regional variations emerged in

Plate XV: Small polychrome glazed baked clay jar; western Iran; c. 800–700 BC; Ht. 0·100 [1971.981]. (*From the collection of Mr. James Bomford.*)

pottery manufacture, possibly as native traditions re-asserted themselves. Among these the pottery of cemetery 'B' at Tepe Sialk, c. 850–650 BC, is outstanding. In the west, growing military and commercial involvement with Assyria and Urartu (modern Armenia) had important cultural effects. Urartu for some time occupied much of Azerbaijan and Assyrian armies drove deep into the Zagros valleys, both to secure their eastern frontier against Urartians and Iranians and to ensure an adequate supply of horses for their armies (pl XIV). Of the native kingdoms that of Mannai,

26

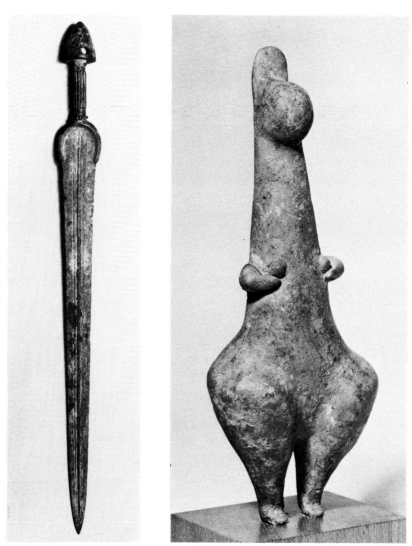

Plate XVI: Bronze sword; north-west Iran; *c.* 1200–1000 BC; L. 0·740 |1965.771|. (*Gift of Mr. James Bomford.*)
Plate XVII: Baked clay statuette of a woman; north-west Iran; *c.* 1200–1000 BC; Ht. 0·197. The authenticity of this figure has been established by a thermoluminescence test [1968.1024]. (*Bomford Trust purchase.*)

27

south of Lake Urmia, is best known from Assyrian and Urartian records; but they say nothing of its origins. It was eventually absorbed by the Medes. The complex of cultures active in Azerbaijan and Kurdistan in the eighth century is strikingly evident in the miscellaneous collection of gold, silver, ivory and glazed pottery objects associated with a 'hoard' found at Ziwiyeh near the

Plate XVIII: Burnished black vessel in the form of a zebu; Gilan; c. 1200–1000 BC; L. 0·260. The authenticity of this vessel has been established by a thermoluminescence test [1964.348].

town of Sakkiz in 1947. In a medley of styles Assyrian, Urartian and Scythian traits are evident, but often executed in a manner which suggests the work of local craftsmen rather than imports.

The problems involved in studying this period are well illustrated in two regions, Gilan (*Amlash*) and Luristan, where chance finds and illicit excavations have revealed a wealth of objects, which proper research is just beginning to set in context. In both regions the range and skill of metalworkers (pl. XVI) is notable; but only in Gilan is there also a marked flair for potting. The vessels in animal

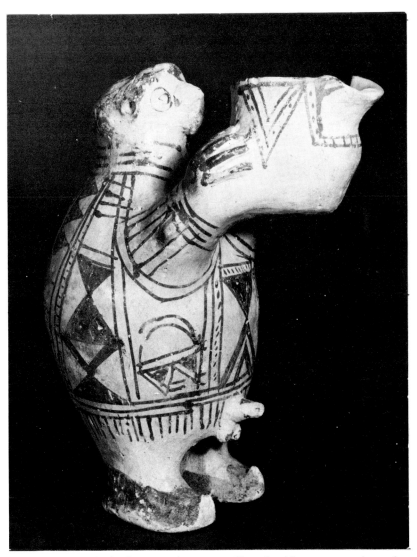

Plate XIX: Baked clay vessel, cream slipped with orange paint, of a naked man pouring a libation; Luristan, *c.* 800–700 BC; a very similar vessel was found at Baba Jan Tepe Ht. 0·242 [1971.982]. (*From the collection of Mr. James Bomford.*)

29

and human form from the richly equipped cemetery of Marlik (Iron I), and also from many unknown sites, in richly burnished wares of dull reddish-brown and grey, have an outstanding sculptural quality (pl. XVIII). Whether the magnificent gold vessels found also at Marlik are local products, or imports from the west, has yet to be

Plate XX: Iron bracelet in two sections joined by rivets; Luristan, c. 800 BC; 0·086×0·090 [1972.165]. (*Bomford Trust purchase.*)

resolved. In Luristan native smiths working in an age-old tradition, given sudden prosperity and independence by exceptional economic and political conditions, created a whole range of elaborately decorated bronze weapons, horse-harness, idols, pins and personal ornaments, and pioneered the use of iron (pls. XX, XXI). Naturalistically modelled animals are juxtaposed to demons, half-man, half-beast, cast, or incised on sheetmetal, in a highly stylised fashion. Without written records the myths they illustrate remain as enigmatic as their makers are anonymous.

30

It is only when the Iranian-speaking peoples appear in Assyrian state records, the Persians in 844 BC, the Medes in 836 BC, that a coherent picture gradually emerges. At this time the Persians were established, in part at least, somewhere in Kurdistan; by soon after 700 BC they were far to the south-east in modern Fars (Persis),

Plate XXI: Bronze ring for a horse's headstall—mouflon and lions; Luristan c. 800–700 BC; 0·086×0·084 [1965.196]. (*From the collection of the late Captain E. G. Spencer-Churchill.*)

encroaching eastwards into Elam. The Medes, with their Scytho-Cimmerian confederates, were grouped round a capital at Ecbatana (Hamadan) on the eastern end of the main route through the central Zagros. In the archaeological record this period (Iron Age III, c. 800–400 BC) is characterised by plain buff pottery, sometimes with incised or painted decoration.

From about 614–610 BC the Medes, in alliance with the Babylonians, overthrew the weakened Assyrian Empire and

Plate XXII: Burnished cream vase in the shape of a boot with decoration in dark paint; north west Iran; Iron III period; Ht. 0·250 [1971.984]. (*From the collection of Mr. James Bomford.*)

marched on into Turkey as far as the Halys river. Then for half a century their history is unknown. Greek authors relate that the subsequent Persian monarchy drew much upon Median custom. The many-columned halls of Persepolis certainly have seventh century precursors at Godin Tepe and Nush-i Jan in Media. Of two fire-temples at Nush-i Jan one was systematically packed from floor to ceiling with rubble, perhaps when its sacred fire was ritually extinguished at a king's death.

To this period the great Iranian prophet Zarathushtra (Greek Zoroaster) is traditionally dated. He lived in eastern Iran. His teachings have survived in some of his hymns (the *Gathas*), which, though revealing a knowledge of the traditional mythology of the Aryans, give a profoundly philosophical interpretation of the Universe. He proclaimed a single supreme God, creator of all things, beyond the reach of evil forces. The world is divided between two opposite poles of Good and Evil, Truth and Lie, offered as free choices to all humanity. The supreme symbol of Truth is fire and fire-altars are consequently the primary cult symbol of Zoroastrianism.

VIII. The Empire of the Achaemenid Kings c. 550–330 BC

Iran fully entered world history under the Persian King Cyrus 'the Great' (c. 559–530 BC), descendant of Achaemenes (c. 700–675 BC?). His father, king of Anshan in Fars, had married the Median king's daughter. Cyrus seized his grandfather's throne, welded the Medes and Persians into a coherent state and fully exploited the fine army he had inherited, first to cross the Halys river in Turkey and defeat the legendary Croesus, King of Lydia, then to unseat the unpopular Nabonidus, King of Babylon. There in 538 BC he achieved enduring fame in western tradition by releasing the Jews from captivity and authorising the rebuilding of the Temple in Jerusalem. Upon the basis he established his immediate successors, outstandingly Darius I (c. 522–486 BC), created the greatest of all ancient Near Eastern Empires, extending from the Aegean to the Indus, from Arabia to the Caucasus. The famous inscription at Behistun describes the accession of Darius, the Apadana friezes at

Plate XXIII: Modern impressions from a stamp-seal with designs on both faces and two sides: an Achaemenid king triumphant and various motifs of religious significance, to right Ahuramazda in a disk above on altar; bought in Beirut, Lebanon; 5th to 4th centuries BC; 0·040×0·030×0·017 [1889.406].

34

Persepolis illustrate the tribute peoples of his Empire. Greek historians, notably Herodotus (*c.* 480–425 BC) and Xenophon (*c.* 430–355 BC), who served Cyrus 'the Younger' as a mercenary, wrote accounts of the Persians that have been widely supplemented by more recent discoveries of public and private documents of the time written in Old Persian, Elamite, Akkadian, Aramaic, Hebrew and Egyptian.

Plate XXIV: Modern impression from an Achaemenid cylinder seal showing two priests officiating at a fire-altar; bought in Egypt; 5th to 4th centuries BC; 0·034×0·013 [1892.1416].

As the home of the ruling dynasty Iran held a privileged position in the Empire, but it was in the modern sense something of an underdeveloped country, eclipsed by the wealthy provinces of Egypt, Phoenicia and Babylonia, and the ancient kingdoms of Lydia and Phrygia in Turkey, with their long-established political, social and economic institutions. Archaeological research in Iran has been virtually confined to the palaces of Susa, which shared with Babylon administrative control of the Empire; to Pasargadae, the coronation city of the dynasty founded by Cyrus I; and to Persepolis, creation of Darius I, whither the monarchs came in life on fixed occasions to celebrate the achievements of their ancestors through religious

35

Plate XXVa,b: Cast silver lion-shaped handles and a silver gilt ram's head terminal from a coin hoard buried in northern Turkey about 425 to 420 BC; Ht. 0·040; L. 0·055 [1970.1099a,b, 1970.1098].

36

ceremonies and diplomatic receptions and in death to be buried. Iranian and foreign traditions in art and architecture were skilfully fused through specialist craftsmen drawn from all over the empire. They produced a court style, on glazed brick and sculptured friezes, entirely distinctive of the new imperial overlords, though using the traditional iconography of the superseded Assyrian and Babylonian kings. Throughout the empire there was a wide degree of religious tolerance; but persisting uncertainty surrounds the religion of the Great King and his court (pl. XXIV). Some have seen elements of

Plate XXVI: Shallow silver dish (Phiale) with fluted decoration; source unknown; 5th century BC; D. 0·172 [1971.988]. (*From the collection of Mr. James Bomford.*)

Zoroastrianism in the inscriptions of Darius, but others date royal acceptance of Zoroaster's teachings to the reign of Artaxerxes I, *c.* 441 BC, when the civil calendar was reformed with months named after leading Zoroastrian deities.

Throughout the Empire the presence of rich patrons attached to the courts of the local governors (satraps) stimulated local craftsmen to adjust their traditional skills and styles to the new taste in gold and silver plate, jewellery, fine cut-glass and pottery vessels, particularly to the Iranian love of animal ornament and colour contrasts (pl. XXVa, b). Even so local preferences often emerge, particularly in Egypt and Turkey where deepseated artistic traditions asserted themselves (pl. XXVII). The renowned 'Treasure of the Oxus' in the British Museum provides a microcosm of Achaemenid craftsmanship in gold and silver. It was discovered in uncertain circumstances on the banks of the river Oxus in 1877 and may have come originally from a temple.

Though concealed by the forceful character and energy of its founders the Achaemenid Empire was dangerously unstable in the hands of lesser rulers, for so much depended on the king. After about 450 BC court intrigues regularly endangered the succession,

Plate XXVII: Silver goblet in a Greco-Persian style from western Turkey; 5th century BC, Ht. 0·080 [1967.819]. (*Bomford Trust purchase.*)

which had never been secure. Sporadic conflict in the west with Greece, in the east with nomadic intruders, and the ambitions of powerful satraps with private armies, constantly threatened to break the Empire up. Alexander the Great of Macedon caught it at a particularly weak moment and with the skill and energy of genius exploited its divisions to secure for himself, very briefly, an even

38

greater dominion. Whether he burnt Persepolis in 330 BC at the whim of a courtesan Thäis in a fit of drunken wrath, or as calculated revenge for the Persian sack of Athens in 480 BC, the act sensationally marked for all time the end of the ancient Near Eastern empires; inspiring at least one English Literary masterpiece:

> '...Behold how they toss their torches on high,
> How they point to the Persian abodes
> And glittering temples of their hostile gods.
> —The princes applaud with a furious joy:
> And the King seized a flambeau with zeal to destroy;
>> Thäis led the way
>> To light him to his prey,
> And like another Helen, fired another Troy!'

John Dryden (1631–1700): *Alexander's Feast*.

IX. The Age of Foreign Rulers: Seleucids and Parthians, *c.* 323 BC to AD 240

From the death of Alexander to the accession of Ardashir nearly six hundred years later the course of events in Iran is known primarily from the writings of Greco-Roman authors, sparsely supplemented from local excavations. In Iran inscriptions are rare and the historical evidence to be drawn from coins is sparse. Much has still to be inferred from the evidence of excavations in the Seleucid and Parthian cities of Iraq, where the administrative capitals lay, or in important provincial centres to the east now in the U.S.S.R. or Afghanistan.

Much of Iran was only sporadically under the control of the dynasty founded by Alexander's general Seleucus, who between *c.* 312 and 302 BC established himself and his family as rulers over much of Alexander's eastern Empire. In all vital respects the organisation and administrative methods of the Achaemenids survived, albeit increasingly Hellenised. Seleucid rule was secured through the foundation of cities, or Greek military colonies, along the main lines of communication, notably the great Khorasan road to independent Bactria, a focal point of Greek influence in the east. The impact of Greek language and script, and Greek culture, was subtle and more pervasive.

In cities where Greeks were most in evidence art and architecture was deeply affected by pure Greek forms, but further afield native traditions persisted side-by-side with hybrids of new and old. In religion also, for the Seleucids were tolerant of local cults, a similar pattern is evident. Greek gods, especially Heracles, were regularly identified with native deities. There is still a crudely cut rock-relief of the reclining Heracles at Behistun; fragments of a monumental bronze statue, possibly of Antiochus IV (*c.* 176–163 BC), and metal figurines of gods, from a temple at Shami in Khuzistan are Greek in

40

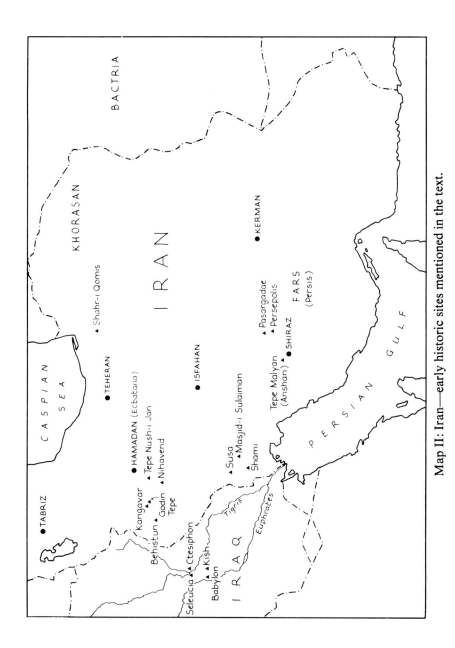

Map II: Iran—early historic sites mentioned in the text.

Plate XXVIII: Bronze censer, said to be from Iran, showing a reclining male banqueteer; Parthian period; L. 0.242 [1971.971]. (*From the collection of Mr. James Bomford.*)

style. Most of what survives of temples on platforms at sites like Kangavar in Kurdistan and Masjid-i-Sulaiman in Khuzistan seems to be Parthian rather than Seleucid, though the foundations were Seleucid.

The Seleucids, long harassed by revolts in their more easterly provinces, were finally overthrown by tribesmen from the region of modern Khorasan and beyond, ancient Parthia. Russian excavations at Old Nisa, funerary city of the early Parthian rulers, have revealed spacious buildings, among them a theatre of Greek type, fine ivory objects sometimes carved with scenes from Greek myth, and many administrative documents. Parthian rule over Iran, and further west, was ensured by the campaigns of Mithradates I (*c.* 171–138 BC), though their position in Iran was not secured for another half-century. Even then constant pressure from Rome in the west, the Kushans in the east, offered regular opportunities to ambitious vassals or provincial governors. Nomadic in origin the Parthians accepted the Hellenised organs of government and administration surviving from the Achaemenid period. But in time the demands of unruly feudal lords modified them. The army, with greatly expanded cavalry detachments, was forged into an instrument feared even by the Romans. Wealth accrued from the overland trade with China, and sea borne commerce up the Persian Gulf, that brought spices and oriental luxuries westwards to markets in the Roman Empire.

The Parthian cities of Iran, traditionally circular in plan, have been little explored; only at Shahr-i Qomis (the ancient Parthian capital of Hecatompylos?) have excavations begun to reveal a city in many respects parallel to sites of the period excavated by the Russians far to the east in central Asia. The few surviving rock-reliefs are ill-executed and awkwardly arranged, whether scenes of homage or royal victory, as at Behistun for Mithradates II (123–88/87 BC) and Gotarzes II (*c.* AD 38–51), or individual figures at worship besides fire-altars. A magnificent, over life-size figure of a Parthian ruler from Shami is still an isolated indication of what may remain to be discovered. Bronze censers (pl. XXVIII) and terracotta figurines more often evoke for us the major arts of a people whose nomadic traditions blended distinctively with the varied Greco-Roman stylistic influences by now current in Iran. About this time the Iranian national epic, the 'Book of Kings' (*Shāh-nāma*), was first assembled into coherent form.

X. The Sasanian Empire, *c.* AD 240 to 642

Throughout the period of foreign domination the old Achaemenid imperial traditions, and native Iranian aspirations, had been maintained in the province of *Persis*. In the new provincial capital of Istakhr, near Persepolis, the hereditary chief-priest of Anahita's temple, descendant of one Sasan, exercised some secular authority. From his family came Ardashir, first of the Sasanian kings (AD 22?–40), who, in circumstances obscured by later legends, overthrew the last of the Parthian rulers. His successor Shahpur I (AD 240 to 272?) drove with his armies westwards to Syria and Cappadocia, eastwards into India. Links with the Achaemenid past were consciously revived and royal authority directed to the creation of a highly centralised administration capable of effecting systematic programmes of town-building, irrigation and industrialisation. Religious policy was no less authoritarian and conservative. Orthodox Zoroastrianism was enforced as the state religion and numerous minority cults were persecuted.

Sufficient survives of Sasanian cities and palaces, only a few yet partially excavated, sculptures, coins and such minor objects as seals and silver plate, to offer a more reliable account of their artistic achievements in Iran than is yet possible with their immediate predecessors. In palace architecture the *iwan**, developed by Parthian builders, was exploited widely in combination with square, domed rooms and vaulted halls around large courtyards. Stucco, particularly distinctive of Sasanian art, was used on walls and vaults to form panelled friezes or elaborate geometrical patterns, of symbols and monograms, of royal busts (Frontispiece) and more extended scenes. In these, as in the better-known royal rock-reliefs and on silver bowls, the ancient Near Eastern motifs of

---

*A high, barrel-vaulted, rectangular room, enclosed on three sides, opening on the fourth onto a courtyard.

Plate XXIX: Gilt bronze terminal on the iron shaft; a prince's or male deity's head; source within Iran uncertain; late Parthian or Sasanian period; Ht. 0·085 [1971.970]. (*From the collection of Mr. James Bomford.*)

45

the royal hunt, the investiture of a king or his triumphs in battle predominate. Numerous stamp-seals and seals for setting in ring-bezels, carved in a variety of coloured stones, either bear miniature versions of the same scenes (pl. XXX) or just rudely cut monograms, or animals. Fragments of decorated Sasanian silks preserved in the monasteries of western Europe, whither they

Plate XXX: Modern impression from a Sasanian stamp-seal showing a royal 'investitute' scene, with a recumbent man beneath; 5th century AD; bought in Egypt. 0·027×0·022 [1889.572].

travelled across the Byzantine Empire (whose artists imitated them for centuries), lend life and colour to the richly patterned garments carved in detail on the great late Sasanian rock-reliefs at Taq-i Bostan in Kurdistan.

In the sixth century the Sasanian Empire reached a peak of achievement in the reign of Khusrau I (AD 531–79), whose reputation passed into legend as the hero who would return at the end of the world to save Iran. Yet, as in the Achaemenid Empire, internal and external pressures were manifold. Rivalry between the

Sasanian and Byzantine Empires had long been acute when under Khusrau II (AD 591–628) Iranian troops marched as far as Alexandria in Egypt and in Jerusalem seized the Holy Cross as a trophy. The Byzantine Emperor Heraclius counter-attacked with a brilliant campaign through the Caucasus into the heart of the Sasanian Empire. Khusrau's generals revolted, the king was killed, and rulers followed in quick succession. But it was not to Byzantium that the Sasanian Empire fell. A mutual foe, potentially greater than both, struck with meteoric force. The nomad tribes of Arabia united as never before by a new religious fervour swept through Syria and Iraq, finally breaking what remained of Sasanian power at the battle of Nihavend in western Iran in AD 642. The military victory was swift and decisive, but the deep-seated traditions of Iran and its formidable geography to this day temper the full impact of Islam.

Concise Bibliography

Although this list is intentionally confined to reasonably accessible books in English, many of them have bibliographies which will take the reader deeper into the literature of the subject. Asterisks denote the existence of paperback editions.

GENERAL

A. J. Arberry (Ed)., *The Legacy of Persia*, Oxford, 1963.

W. B. Fisher (Ed.), *The Land of Iran*, Cambridge History of Iran, I, Cambridge, 1968.

R. Levy, *The Epic of the Kings, Shah-nama*, London, 1967.

*S. A. Matheson, *Persia: an Archaeological Guide*, London, 1972.

*H. E. Wulff, *The Traditional Crafts of Persia*, Cambridge, Mass., 1967.

PRIMARILY HISTORY AND ARCHAEOLOGY

C. G. Cameron, *History of Early Iran*, Chicago, 1936.

M. A. R. Colledge, *The Parthians*, London, 1967.

W. Culican, *The Medes and Persians*, London, 1965.

R. N. Frye, *The Heritage of Persia*, London, 1962.

*R. Ghirshman, *Iran, from the Earliest Times to the Islamic Conquest*, London, Penguin Books, 1961.

E. Herzfeld, *Iran in the Ancient East*, London, 1941.

W. Hinz, *The Lost World of Elam*, London, 1972.

*A. T. Olmstead, *History of the Persian Empire*, Chicago, 1948.

also the relevant sections of the *Revised Cambridge Ancient History*, vols. I and II.

PRIMARILY ART AND ARCHAEOLOGY

A. D. H. Bivar, *Catalogue of the Western Asiatic Seals in the British Museum. Stamp Seals II: The Sassanian Dynasty*, London, 1969.

48

R. Ghirshman, *Iran—from the Origins to Alexander the Great*, London, 1964.

Iran—Parthians and Sassanians, London, 1962.

A. Godard, *The Art of Iran*, London, 1965.

*P. R. S. Moorey, *Ancient Bronzes from Luristan*, British Museum Publications, London, 1974.

Ancient Persian Bronzes in the Adam Collection, London, 1974.

A. U. Pope (Ed.), *A Survey of Persian Art from Prehistoric Times to the Present*, Oxford, 1938, vols. I (text), IV (plates).

E. Porada, *Ancient Iran: the Art of Pre-Islamic Times*, London, 1965.

D. N. Wilber, *Persepolis: the Archaeology of Parsa Seat of the Persian Kings*, London, 1969.

RELIGION

J. R. Hinnells, *Persian Mythology*, London, 1973

R. C. Zaehner, *The Dawn and Twilight of Zoroastrianism*, London, 1961.

ADJACENT AREAS

C. Burney and D. M. Lang, *The Peoples of the Hills: Ancient Ararat and Caucasus*, London, 1971.

K. Jettmar, *Art of the Steppes*, London, 1967

S. N. Kramer, *The Sumerians*, Chicago, 1963.

V. M. Masson and V. I. Sariandi, *Central Asia: Turkmenia before the Achaemenids*, London, 1972.

A. L. Oppenheim, *Ancient Mesopotamia*, Chicago, 1964.

Mortimer Wheeler, *Flames over Persepolis*, London, 1968.

ASHMOLEAN COLLECTION

P. R. S. Moorey, *Catalogue of the Ancient Persian Bronzes in the Ashmolean Museum*, Oxford, 1971.

Current archaelogical research in Iran is regularly reported in *Iran*, Journal of the British Institute of Persian Studies in Teheran.

Index

This index is not comprehensive. It is designed only to assist rapid reference to the text by visitors to the Ashmolean Galleries.

INDEX